Contents

I0409957

Abstract

Increased attention must be directed toward Mexico due to the direct and immediate effects issues like Mexican migration, cross border drug control, and transnational organized crime have on U.S. national security. Two primary issues underpin these shared security issues. These are a weak economy and an inadequate education system. Accordingly, this paper posits a relationship between education, economic health, and crime. To be specific, by strengthening the education system, Mexico's economy will improve. Together, these conditions will augment the government's ability to counter criminal activity. To illuminate this topic further, the first section of the paper substantiates a relationship between education, the economy, and crime. The second section then justifies U.S. involvement, and the third and final section details recommended focus areas to bolster the Mexican education system.

INTRODUCTION

MEXICO: THE SPILLOVER EFFECT ON U.S. NATIONAL SECURITY

Countries like Afghanistan, Iraq, Yemen, and Syria remain at the forefront of United States national security concerns, especially since September 11, 2001. Yet, increased attention must be directed toward Mexico due to the direct and immediate effects issues like Mexican migration, cross border drug control, and transnational organized crime have on U.S. national security. According to a Council on Foreign Relations report on Transnational Crime, U.S. Border Security, and the War on Drugs in Mexico, "Mexican drug traffickers are the single greatest domestic organized crime threat within the U.S., operating in every state and hundreds of U.S. cities, selling uncontrolled substances that directly endanger the health and safety of millions of ordinary citizens."[1] Further exacerbating the threat to U.S. national security is the large number of illegal Mexican immigrants coming to the U.S., accounting for sixty-two percent of the total number of illegal immigrants within the U.S..[2] Some of these immigrants come to the U.S. to escape drug trafficking organizations.[3] Alternatively, there are others who seek to escape poor economic conditions within Mexico.[4] Compounding this issue is the fact that 18.2 percent of the Mexican population live below the poverty line.[5]

Two primary issues underpin these shared security concerns. These are a weak economy and an inadequate education system. Mexico's weak economy limits legitimate income sources/opportunities and paves the way for illegal economic activities like drug production and drug trafficking.[6] Moreover, Mexico's education system is plagued by high dropout rates and yields students who perform far below average when compared to other Organization for Economic Co-operation and Development (OECD) member countries.[7]

Therefore, in acknowledgment of the negative spillover effect transnational organized crime and a weak Mexican economy can have on U.S. national security, the following must be accomplished. With the support of the U.S., the Government of Mexico's (GOM) must continue refinement of education policies aimed at improving the qualification of teachers and those that promote completion of lower and upper secondary school. Together, these efforts will enhance the country's ability to establish a strong economic foundation and augment their ability to counter criminal activity.

The relationship between education and the economy is widely accepted and often addressed in public forums, like the U.S. President's speech on August 10, 2010 calling for the U.S. to strive to become the world leader in college graduates by 2020, without which the future competitiveness of the U.S. was at stake.[8] Yet, not all agree with this relationship and often contest it, claiming it is the result of faulty logic. As an example, an article in the Las Vegas Review Journal states, "if higher education can't explain why some states struggle and others are recovering, we can't say with any certainty that higher education will be an engine of economic development -- especially if higher education doesn't evolve and innovate. At worst, spending more money to achieve the same results will retard our economic development."[9]

While the argument above seems valid, the author fails to understand that "higher education" doesn't only mean attainment of a higher level of education through money and time; it also implies that the quality and depth of education must also progress. This distinction is significant and serves as a foundational theme throughout the remainder of this paper. More specifically, with regard to Mexico, schools are not built within each community, thus necessitating a two to three hour journey for those in rural areas that would

2

like to attend school.[10] Therefore, the quantity of facilities is of increased importance especially for poor and rural areas. The level of attainment within the educational system is also significant because of the impact higher education has on job congruency, the likelihood an individual will work in the same field they received specialized training in, thus affecting the type of job, productivity level, and wage earning capacity.[11] Nevertheless, this emphasis on the number of educational facilities and number of years of education does not diminish the importance of the quality of the educational system at large. These and other issues such as the correlation between education and the economy will be addressed in depth during the remainder of the paper.

HISTORICAL REVIEW OF MEXICO'S EDUCATION SYSTEM
AND POLICIES

If the significant gains in Mexico's enrollment system over the last forty years (9.7 million in 1970 to 21.6 million students in 2000) also signified expansive progression in education level, quality of education, and student test scores (e.g., Science, Reading and Math), the Mexican education system would likely rival that of countries like Korea, Belgium, and Sweden.[12] Yet, despite increased funding and implementation of a number of educational reform policies, student performance is far below the OECD average, thus signifying a need for further modifications to the educational system. [13]

Specific to educational funding, compared to the average 13.3 percent of total public expenditure OECD countries spend on education, Mexico spends 22 percent, more than any other OECD country.[14] While significant in terms of Mexico's public expenditure, the actual expendinture per student in dollar terms is approximately $1,350 (U.S.) compared to the OECD average of $8,857.[15] Furthermore, this figure is disproportionately spent such that the

3

lower, primary levels receive less ($800) than upper secondary levels ($1,700), while higher education levels (~$4,000) receive the preponderance of funding. This funding allocation is unusual not only because of the large increase in higher education funding, but also because the GoM's compulsory educational system is only comprised of grades one through nine. If funding corresponds to level of importance, the government places a high priority on higher education, but less importance on the foundational and prerequisite educational levels. This disparity also exists between rural (low-income) and urban (higher-income) areas, further limiting the pool of people with sufficient qualifications or access to higher educational opportunities.[16]

Overall, while Mexico's interest in improving the education system is evident via increased funding allocations, shortfalls remain. More specifically, of the funding allocated for primary and secondary education levels, the majority is allocated toward teacher/staff compensation, thus limiting the amount that can be directed toward instructional materials. On average, this amounts to 5.6 percent of the allocated budget, vice the OECD country average expenditure of 19 percent.[17] Of course, this is not to say that teachers in Mexico receive higher than average salaries; rather, the converse is true. For comparison, the OECD average salary for primary school teachers is $41 per hour, lower secondary teachers receive $51/hour, and upper secondary teachers receive $59/hour. On the other hand, teachers in Mexico receive on average approximately $21/hour.[18]

Independent school funding is yet another funding shortfall. While the percentage of government expenditure on education as a whole is above the OECD country average, independent school budgets are non-existent for those who do not have the administrative capacity to complete the application process and close to non-existent even for those that do.

As a result, the schools with the greatest need, those in rural areas, tend to receive even less.[19]

In regard to educational infrastructure, the government sponsored education system continues to fall short of the overall country-wide requirement. Aside from the differences in the number of facilities between rural and urban areas, of the educational facilities available, many do not have basic infrastructure such as bathrooms, cement floors, student desks, and blackboards. Of the schools that do have these basics, they usually do not have physical education, arts, or music facilities, while computers and internet access are extremely rare (of the existing schools, only six percent have computer and internet access).[20]

With respect to educational reform, Mexico has implemented a number of substantial and positive policies over the last 50 years, one of the more significant being enactment of an eleven year compulsory education mandate to improve educational quality and attendence.[21] The Mexican educational system has four main levels consisting of preschool (ages three through five), compulsory basic education (primary, grades one through six, and lower secondary, grades seven through nine), upper secondary (grades ten through twelve), and higher education.[22] Compulsory education is comprised of grades one through nine, but implementation of a 2009 law will add preschool to the list starting in 2012. The government funds and manages the compulsory education program through the Secretaria de Educación (SEP), which establishes the curriculum, selects the text books, and manages the teaching staff.[23] While not officially responsible for the remaining levels of education, as shown by Mexico's funding levels, the government's primary focus is on the upper education levels. Moreover, in acknowledgement of the importance of educating the Mexican populace,

Article 3 of the Mexican Constitution was modified in 2000 to stipulate that all individuals have a right to education.[24]

Despite Mexico's increased focus on education and implementation of a compulsory education system, Mexican students still perform in the lower category when compared to other OECD countries. More specifically, according to a 2006 OECD Programme for International Student Assessment on math, reading and science, the median score for Mexican students was 410 points, well below the OECD average of 500 points. While they outperformed countries like Kyrgizstan (322 points), Qatar (349 points), and Tunisia (386 points), they fell far short of competing with other countries like the U.S. (489 points), Canada (534 points), and Korea (522 points).[25]

In addition to Mexico's compulsory education program, Mexico also implemented standardized national admission and exit examinations. This education policy was originally initiated as a means to reduce the disparity in the "measurement of professional quality" and was instigated as a result of the North American Free Trade Agreement (NAFTA).[26] In essence, if Mexico was to compete with the U.S. and Canada on somewhat of an equal footing, common criteria for professional services (e.g., doctors, nurses, engineers) needed to be established. While Mexico's rationale for implementing standardized admissions and exit examinations is sound, overall this initiative seems to have fallen short of the original objective. In particular, the tests themselves were built based on national standards that were and still remain ill defined. Additionally, test development appeared to have occurred in a vacuum, no coordination occurred between the test and the curriculum developers. Hence, a disparity existed between what students were being taught and what they were being tested on. The test is also multiple choice, thus there is no ability to test a student's problem solving skills.[27] These shortfalls diminish the credibility of these tests when compared to a broad base like the OECD countries at large.

Another educational reform initiative was the establishment of teacher evaluations and professional development mechanisms. The overarching goal of any teacher evaluation program is to improve student learning outcomes. This is accomplished through establishment of criteria for good teaching practices, establishment of basic education level qualifications, and mandatory subject matter knowledge skills. Teachers can then be evaluated based on overall student performance, tests for the teachers themselves, student assessments, surveys, etc.[28] Mexico implemented this program in 1999 as a means to ensure teachers were qualified to teach the subject matter. Yet, the student curriculum was modified as early as 1993, thus leaving a six year gap where teachers were likely unqualified to teach the new curriculum due to the lack of initial teacher training. Today, years after implementation of the program, only 60 percent of the teachers have attended a teacher education institution, leaving 40 percent without any prepatory training to teach, no accreditation standards to comply with, and no quality control mechanism.[29]

In addition to the shortfall in teacher qualifications and competency in the subject matter, a single, standardized, in-service teacher evaluation program is not currently available in Mexico, nor is it currently feasible. Within the state of Chiapas alone there are six indigenous languages, 56 percent of the localities have less than 500 people, and the majority of schools have only one teacher.[30] Considering there are 30 other states, it is unlikely a single teacher evaluation system can be implemented in Mexico, thus increasing the difficulty in baselining the content of what is taught within the government standardized curriculum.

Mexico's realization of the importance of education is evidenced by the significant amount of funding they allocate to this effort as well as their implementation of educational reform policies. All efforts are aimed at improving the quality and reach of educational programs within Mexico. Yet, even with this increased emphasis, Mexico falls short in one of the single most important indicators of effectiveness, student performance results. Mexican student test results still fall well below the OECD average. Therefore, although Mexico has made significant strides in providing educational opportunities to Mexican citizens, there is still a tremendous amount that can and must be done to improve the educational system, thus making it competitive not just within Mexico itself, but on a world scale.

THE LINK BETWEEN EDUCATION AND THE ECONOMY

Economic well being and a solid educational system are two issues governments must remain well attuned to in order to sustain or gain a competitive standing in the world market. Yet, if a relationship between the two is substantiated, governments may be able to positively affect one by improving the other. Indeed, there is a correlation between the economy and education, and to illustrate the relationship the following three factors will be used: labor quality via educational achievement, salary differential, and job congruency.

The first factor is the notion that the quality of human labor is improved through education, thereby improving productivity. The 2011 OECD Economic Survey on Mexico describes this correlation by first addressing the extensive "informal sector" in Mexico. The informal secor is comprised of firms that do not conform to tax and labor laws. These informal firms are typically small (to hide their activities), unproductive (since they do not have access to formal resources such as loans, a large customer base, and training), and they tend to hire unskilled laborers because they cannot compete with formal firms in the skilled labor market.[31] The report contends that these informal firms hinder overall productivity and growth. Therefore, in Mexico's case, development of policies designed to reduce barriers to entry into the formal economy, those designed to improve the quality and depth of technical training and education overall, will minimize the advantages of moving into or remaining within the informal market. The overall objective is to reduce or eliminate the informal network, while expanding the formal economy. Together, productivity should increase, as should tax income and the economy overall.[32]

To further emphasize the impact education has on economic well being, the salaries of individuals with higher versus lower or no prior education were analyzed. According to Gladys López-Acevedo, Senior Economist in the Poverty and Gender Group at the World Bank in the Latin American Region, education accounts for the largest disparity in wage earnings within Mexico even though education attainment overall has increased over time.[33] The more education attained, the higher the wage. In her study, Lopez-Acevedo uses a number of formulas and models to substantiate the high rate of return in terms of wage earnings when compared to education levels.[34] The study concludes that "education is the most important variable in the explanation of earnings inequality."

In addition to López-Acevedo's findings, the issue of salary differential has been evaluated in a number of other venues including a study by Yolanda K. Kodrzycki, a senior economist director of the New England Public Policy Center at the Federal Reserve Bank of Boston. Kodrzycki's work, titled, "Educational Attainment as a Constraint on Economic Growth and Social Progress," analyzed the schooling variances between whites, blacks, and Hispanics in relation to their wage earnings. Her findings detail a distinct difference based on quality of schooling versus quantity of schooling between the groups. She also notes a positive correlation between the educational achievements of children and the educational achievements of their parents. This link implies that in order to make a positive impact on the educational deficits for racial and ethnic minorities, a long-term commitment is required.[35] Kodrzycki's findings are reinforced by a report by Hanushek and Wößmann that, "the cognitive skills of a population– rather than mere school attainment – are powerfully related to individual earnings, to the distribution of income, and to economic growth."[36] More specifically, while there is a positive correlation between school quantity and economic growth, the true catalyst to economic growth is the quality of the education. Therefore, while higher education expands the type and depth of knowledge, increased focus on the quality of all levels of education is essential.

Job congruency is yet another factor signifying a correlation between education and economics. Job congruency is the likelihood an individual will work in the same field in which they received specialized training. To illustrate job congruency, a study of Mexico's largest technical education institute, Colegio Nacional de Educación Profesional Técnica (CONALEP), performed by López-Acevedo is referrenced. In her study, López-Acevedo analyzed CONALEP 1991 graduates with a control group in relation to job attainment post graduation. While members of the control group were able to acquire jobs at a faster pace than CONALEP graduates, a larger number of CONALEP graduates worked within their field of training and earned wages that were on average 20 to 28 percent higher than those within the control group. [37] The study implies a correlation between focused, higher level education and the type and quality of jobs procurred. Simply stated, economic benefits can be attained through education.

One of the most important, yet difficult tasks for a nation's government is to lay the foundation for a healthy economy. Yet, with the knowledge that labor quality, salary differential, and job congruency reinforce the notion of a relationship between education and economic health, governments are now armed with additional alternatives in addressing this difficult task.

THE LINK BETWEEN CRIME, ECONOMY, AND EDUCATION

The influence of crime on the economy appears obvious in that it inhibits the ability to accurately assess individual earnings, thereby negatively affecting the government's ability to tax those earnings. Yet, the link between crime and education may not be as apparent. In fact, crime and education are linked such that a targetted effort aimed at improving the educational system has the potential of mitigating an individual's tendency to choose or be forced into a life of crime. This knowledge provides governments other options to use in the fight against crime.

The relationship between the three factors, crime, education, and the economy, is best illustrated by examining Mexico's drug sector. According to Dr. David A. Shirk, Director of the Transborder Institute and Associate Professor at the University of San Diego, Mexico's drug sector is largely comprised of young, 18-35 year old males who have resorted to the illicit drug business because other economic or educational opportunities were not available to them.[38] Similarly, within the U.S. approximately 75 percent of those in state prisons and 59 percent of those in federal prisons were high school drop outs.[39] These statistics suggest three alternatives for combating crime, increasing the police force, modifying correctional facility methods, and/or improving education. Giving each an equal weight in terms of effectivness and applying an economic perspective to each, there may be a cost savings by

11

focusing on one alternative over another. More specifically, a report titled "Allocating Resources among Prisons and Social Programs in the Battle against Crime," argues that it would be less costly and just as effective to improve the quality of pre-school education programs vice funneling money into the prison system.[40] Similarly, another report, "The Effect of Education on Crime: Evidence from Prison Inmates, Arrests, and Self-Reports," advocates the funding advantages of improving high school graduation rates to counter crime instead of adding to the size of the police force.[41] With this in mind, a review of allocated funds between the three alternatives from 1980 to 2005, one notes that expenditure on education rose by a factor of 1.2, police and law enforcement by a factor of 1.5, and correction facilities funding was tripled.[42] Given crime rates did not diminish over this time, these funding statistics may reinforce the need to rebalance funding to exploit the advantages of education, to improve economic well being, and to spur a reduction in crime.

Additional studies advocating a relationship between crime, education, and the economy utilize economic models to simulate the decision cycle of a rational individual confronted with the choice of legitimate employment, or crime. They conclude that through education, rewards, punishment, and perceived advantages associated with each alternative can be manipulated to increase the likelihood of choosing a legitimate work source and down playing the likelihood of resorting to crime.[43]

The relationship between crime, education, and the economy can seem mystifying, yet, it is elementary. One generally expects education to influence decision processes; therefore, it is not difficult to discern a relationship between education and its ability to shape one's decision to opt for a legitimate course of work vice a life of crime. And, since criminal behavior has a direct impact on the economy in terms of misrepresenting an individual's taxable earnings, as well as the associated costs to counter crime itself, it is conceivable that governments could use this knowledge in modifying their approach in their efforts to counter criminal activity.

WHY THE U.S. SHOULD ASSIST MEXICO IN THE DEVELOPMENT OF EDUCATION POLICY

Given the correlation between education, crime, and the economy, and considering Mexico can exploit this relationship without U.S. intervention, why should the U.S. assist Mexico in the development of education policy? The answer is straightforward. By helping Mexico, the U.S. helps itself. Three specific U.S. advantages include a potential reduction in transborder crime, likelihood of improvement in economic health, and the possibility of a decline in the number of illegal immigrants to the U.S.

First, with regard to the spillover of crime from Mexico, the U.S. is the largest consumer of illicit drugs, thus providing the biggest demand signal for the Mexican drug market. The Mexican drug trade provides an estimated 80 percent of the methamphetamine within the U.S, 15,800 tons of cannabis, and 149 tons of heroin.[44] To combat this trade, the U.S. spends more than $3 billion per year on border patrols alone, a figure that pales in comparison to the lost revenue in legitimate trade along with the associated costs involved with the judicial system and incarceration.[45] Last of all, extreme violence fueled by organized crime results in tens of thousounds of deaths within Mexico and hundreds of deaths within the U.S..[46] All together, the effects on U.S. national security, the U.S. economy, and the U.S. population are significant, thus mandating U.S. intervention.

In regard to improving economic well being, the U.S. funneled over $95.6 billion of foreign direct investment into the Mexican economy just in 2008 and continues to be the largest foreign investor today.[47] Mexico is ranked third amongst all other U.S. trading partners, while the U.S. is ranked first for Mexico. In particular, 80 percent of Mexico's exports are for the U.S., with oil and gas comprising 12 percent.[48] Aside from trade and foreign direct investment, the economic relationship between the U.S. and Mexico extends beyond these quantitative estimates due to the shared 2,000 mile border, migration, tourism, environmental issues, transborder infectious disease control, counter narcotics activities, etc., which all affect the economies of both nations.[49] In addition, assisting Mexico in their educational policy development helps in strengthening the Mexican government, thus enhancing their ability to manage security issues within their country and mitigating spillover effects to the U.S.

The final argument to substantiate U.S. support of GoM educational policy development is the potential to reduce the rate of illegal immigration to the U.S., thus mitigating the impact to the economy and welfare of its citizens. According to a Congressional Budget Office report on immigration, 62 percent of the illegal immigrants or "unauthorized citizens" come from Mexico, approximately 10.8 million people.[50] The economic impact these immigrants have on federal, state, and local government spending vary by source, with some arguing the tax revenues generated by these immigrants in the long term more than compensates for the costs of services that they use.[51] Yet, not all agree since the impact to spending varies by level of government. For example, social security, food stamps and medicaid are provided by the federal government. Strict regulations govern who receives these services. Whereas, state and local governments are mandated by law to provide services such as health care, education, and law enforcement to all individuals residing in their juridiction, regardless of their citizenship.[52] In acknowledgement of these differences, the one point of commonality may be that a reduction in the number of illegal immigrants would likely reduce angst on both sides. Therefore, since Mexican citizens comprise the largest number of illegal immigrants within the U.S., endeavors to reduce the flow would positively affect U.S. citizens at large. Additional debates abound regarding the reason immigrants come to the U.S., but a common belief is that of economic opportunity. This being the case, improving Mexico's economic well being should mitigate the incentive to come to the U.S. As an example, the recent lull in the numbers of illegal Mexican immigrants is being lauded as a result of the poor economic opportunities within the U.S. and a slight boom in economic growth within Mexico. In other words, life in Mexico is more appealing than the dangerous and costly treck to the U.S., resulting in a downswing in the overall number of immigrants coming into the U.S.[53]

In recognition of the relationship between crime, the economy, and education, it is well within U.S. national interest to assist Mexico in the development of educational policy. In particular, U.S. assistance could help in reducing transborder crime, improve economic well being, and reduce the rate of illegal immigration, thus mititaging their effect on U.S. national security.

CONCLUSION AND RECOMMENDATIONS

Mexico's 2,000-mile shared border, common interests with respect to North American competitiveness and trade, transborder infectious diseases control, immigration, tourism, and counterdrug operations, underscore the opportunities and need for the U.S. and Mexico to work together.[54] More specifically, in collaboration with the U.S. the GOM should continue refinement of education policies which will enhance the country's ability to establish a strong economic foundation, thereby augmenting their ability to counter criminal activity. Therefore, in support of shortfalls discovered during research, there are two specific opportunities for the U.S. to engage in education policy development within Mexico. These are, policies aimed at improving the qualification of teachers, and policies aimed at promoting completion of lower and upper secondary school.

First, the U.S. should assist Mexico in the development of policies aimed at improving the qualification of teachers, which in turn affect the education quality for students and enhance their learning outcomes. Policy details must include teacher training, accreditation standards, an evaluation system, and quality controls.[55] Policies of this magnitude will assist Mexico in addressing a recurring shortfall in the quality of their education system and bring them a step closer toward genuine realization of Article 3 of the Mexican Constitution, that all individuals have a right to (quality) education.[56]

Second, the U.S. should assist Mexico in the development of policies which promote completion of lower and upper secondary school. A number of studies from the National Bureau of Economic Research and the Federal Reserve Bank of Boston highlight the utility of incentivizing or "raising the pay-off" of staying within the education system vice dropping out. The studies strongly suggest a correlation between graduation from high school, or upper secondary school in Mexico's case, with higher wage earnings[57] as well as a reduction in the tendency for "crime-prone groups" (high school / upper secondary school aged students) to gravitate toward crime.[58] One of the OECD Economic report indicators further substantiates the need for policies of this nature. Indicator A6 states, "the more educated have a stronger attachment to the labour market," thus amplifying the benefit of additional, quality education.[59] Consequently, development of these types of policies should provide a two-fold benefit, an increase in higher wage-earning-capable students, and two, a decline in the size of the "crime-prone groups," both of which have a complementary effect of enhancing education, improving economic performance through increased productivity, as well as a potential reduction in crime.

Development of these educational policies and attainment of these long-termed goals will require more than assertive foreign policy and polite rhetoric. It will require a strong and continued partnership over the course of many years. Hence, U.S. foresight must remain focused on the positive effects of investment in the Mexican education system and its direct correlation to U.S. national security in order to withstand administration changes and fluctuations in budget strategies.

NOTES

---

[1] David A. Shirk, "The Drug War in Mexico Confronting a Shared Threat." Council on Foreign Relations, Last modified March 2011. Accessed October 12, 2011. i.cfr.org/content/publications/attachments/Mexico_CSR60.pdf.

[2] Nabeel Alsalam and Jonathan Schwabish. "A Description of the Immigrant Population:." Congress of the United States Congressional Budget Office, Last modified June 2011. Accessed October 12, 2022. http://www.cbo.gov/ftpdocs/121xx/doc12168/06-02-Foreign-BornPopulation.pdf.

[3] Shirk, "The Drug War in Mexico Confronting a Shared Threat," 5.

[4] Center for Immigration Studies. "Poverty and Income." Center for Immigration Studies, Accessed October 12, 2011. http://www.cis.org/articles/2001/mexico/poverty.html.

[5] Central Intelligence Agency. "The World Factbook: Mexico." Central Intelligence Agency, Last modified September 27, 2011. Accessed October 12, 2022. https://www.cia.gov/library/publications/the-world-factbook/geos/mx.html.

[6] Shirk, "The Drug War in Mexico Confronting a Shared Threat," 2.

[7] "Education at a Glance 2009: OECD Indicators." Organization for Economic Co-operation and Development, Last modified 2009. Accessed October 11, 2011. http://www.oecd.org/document/24/0,3746,en_2649_39263238_43586328_1_1_1_1,00.html.

[8] Sheryl G. Stolberg, "Obama Calls for U.S. to Lead in Graduation." The New York Times, August 9, 2010. Accessed August 15, 2011. http://www.nytimes.com/2010/08/10/education/10obama.html?adxnnl=1&adxnnlx=1318711313-n9A+Zk63f0wvUouNC+RILg.

[9] Patrick R. Gibbons, "Does higher education drive our economic growth?." Las Vegas Review Journal, February 27, 2011. Accessed August 15, 2011. http://www.lvrj.com/opinion/does-higher-education-drive-our-economic-growth-117005288.html.

[10] Lucrecia Santibañez, Georges Vernez, and Paula Razquin. RAND, "Education in Mexico, Challenges and Opportunities." Last modified 2005. Accessed August 31, 2011. http://www.worldfund.org/assets/files/rand_education%20in%20mexico.pdf.

[11] Gladys López-Acevedo, "Evolution of Earnings and Rates of Returns to Education in Mexico." World Bank, Last modified October 2001. Accessed October 14, 2011. http://www.google.com/url?sa=t&source=web&cd=3&sqi=2&ved=0CC8QFjAC&url=http%3A%2F%2Fciteseerx.ist.psu.edu%2Fviewdoc%2Fdownload%3Fdoi%3D10.1.1.17.6364%26rep%3Drep1%26type%3Dpdf&rct=j&q=Lopez%20Acevedo%20%2B%20education%20to%

20earnings&ei=CsKYTuXHNIWQsQKWnYypCA&usg=AFQjCNHgEaoO1nSzegZ7Z6mtu
lapwXjKFw

[12] Vernez Santibañez and Razquin, "Education in Mexico, Challenges and Opportunities,"
16.

[13] "Education at a Glance 2009: OECD Indicators."Organization for Economic Co-operation
and Development, Last modified 2009. Accessed October 11, 2011.
http://www.oecd.org/document/24/0,3746,en_2649_39263238_43586328_1_1_1_1,00.html.

[14] Ibid., 236.

[15] Ibid., 188.

[16] Vernez Santibañez and Razquin, "Education in Mexico, Challenges and Opportunities,"
12.

[17] Organization for Economic Co-operation and Development. "Policy brief on Mexico:
Education." Organization for Economic Co-operation and Development, Last modified 2006.
Accessed October 14, 2011. www.foropoliticaspublicas.org.mx/docs/Educacion.pdf.

[18] Ibid., 5.

[19] Organization for Economic Co-operation and Development. "OECD Economic Surveys:
Mexico." Organization for Economic Co-operation and Development, Last modified May
2011. Accessed October 14, 2011. http://www.oecd.org/dataoecd/59/58/47875549.pdf.

[20] Vernez Santibañez and Razquin, "Education in Mexico, Challenges and Opportunities,"
32.

[21] Ibid., 71.

[22] Ibid., 6.

[23] Ibid., viii.

[24] Gustavo Guerra "Mexico: Children's Rights – August 2007." Law Library of Congress,
Last modified August 2007. Accessed October 13, 2011. http://www.loc.gov/law/help/child-
rights/pdfs/childrensrights-mexico.pdf.

[25] "Education at a Glance 2009: OECD Indicators."Organization for Economic Co-operation
and Development, 89.

[26] Maria Arriaga Lemus De la Luz, "NAFTA and the Trinational Coalition to Defend Public Education." ResourceLibrary, Last modified October 1999. Accessed October 14, 2011. http://findarticles.com/p/articles/mi_hb3427/is_3_26/ai_n28749669/.

[27] Santibañez, Vernez, and Razquin, "Education in Mexico, Challenges and Opportunities," 102.

[28] Organization for Economic Co-operation and Development. "Towards a Teacher Evaluation Framework in Mexico:." Organization for Economic Co-operation and Development, Last modified December 2009. Accessed October 14, 2011. http://www.oecd.org/dataoecd/35/24/44696802.pdf.

[29] Santibañez, Vernez, and Razquin, "Education in Mexico, Challenges and Opportunities," 31.

[30] Organization for Economic Co-operation and Development. "Towards a Teacher Evaluation Framework in Mexico:." Organization for Economic Co-operation and Development, Last modified December 2009. Accessed October 14, 2011. http://www.oecd.org/dataoecd/35/24/44696802.pdf.

[31] Organization for Economic Co-operation and Development. "OECD Economic Surveys: Mexico." Organization for Economic Co-operation and Development, Last modified May 2011. Accessed October 14, 2011. http://www.oecd.org/dataoecd/59/58/47875549.pdf.

[32] Ibid.

[33] Gladys López-Acevedo,. "Evolution of Earnings and Rates of Returns to Education in Mexico," 40.

[34] Gladys López-Acevedo,. "Evolution of Earnings and Rates of Returns to Education in Mexico," 38.

[35] Yolanda K Kodrzycki, "Educational Attainment as a Constraint on Economic Growth and Social Progress." The Federal Reserve Bank of Boston, Last modified June 2002. Accessed October 14, 2011. http://www.oecd.org/dataoecd/35/24/44696802.pdf.

[36] Eric A Hanushek and Ludger Wößmann. "The Role of Education Quality in Economic Growth." The World Bank, Last modified February 2007. Accessed October 15, 2011. http://library1.nida.ac.th/worldbankf/fulltext/wps04122.pdf.

[37] Gladys López-Acevedo,. "Evolution of Earnings and Rates of Returns to Education in Mexico."

[38] Shirk, "The Drug War in Mexico Confronting a Shared Threat," 2.

[39] Alliance for Excellent Education, "Saving Futures, Saving Dollars The Impact of Education on Crime Reduction and Earnings." Last modified August, 2006. Accessed October 14, 2011. http://www.all4ed.org/files/SavingFutures.pdf

[40] John Donohue and Peter Siegelman. "Allocating Resources among Prisons and Social." Yale Law School, Last modified 1998. Accessed October 15, 2011. http://digitalcommons.law.yale.edu/cgi/viewcontent.cgi?article=1050&context=fss_papers&sei-redir=1&referer=http%3A%2F%2Fwww.google.com%2Fsearch%3Fq%3DJ.%2BDonohue%2BIII%2Band%2BP.%2BSiegelman.%2BAllocating%2BResources%2BAmong%2BPrisons%2Band%2BSocial%2BPrograms%2Binthe%2BBattle%2BAgainst%2BCrime.%26rls%3Dcom.microsoft%3Aen-us%26ie%3DUTF-8%26oe%3DUTF-8%26startIndex%3D%26startPage%3D1#search=%22J.%20Donohue%20III%20P.%20Siegelman.%20Allocating%20Resources%20Among%20Prisons%20Social%20Programs%20inthe%20Battle%20Against%20Crime.%22.

[41] Lance Lochner and Enrico Moretti. "The Effect of Education on Crime: Evidence from Prison Inmates,." Department of Economics, Berkeley, Last modified October 2003. Accessed October 15, 2011. http://www.econ.berkeley.edu/~moretti/lm46.pdf.

[42] Lance Lochner, National Bureau of Economic Research, "Education Policy and Crime." Last modified March, 2010. Accessed August 31, 2011. http://economics.uwo.ca/faculty/lochner/papers/educationpolicycrime_mar10.pdf. (pg 1)

[43] Ibid., 2.

[44] Ross Densley,. "Who's Responsible for U.S. Illegal Drug Traffic." Next Generation Pharmaceutical, Last modified March 18, 2010. Accessed October 15, 2011. http://www.ngpharma.com/news/Whos-responsible-for-US-illegal-drug-traffic/.

[45] Shirk, "The Drug War in Mexico Confronting a Shared Threat," vii.

[46] Ibid., 6.

[47] Angeles Villarreal, "U.S.-Mexico Economic Relations: Trends, Issues, and Implications." Congressional Research Service, Last modified March 31, 2010. Accessed October 16, 2011. http://www.nationalaglawcenter.org/assets/crs/RL32934.pdf.

[48] Ibid.

[49] Ibid.

[50] Ibid.

[51] Melissa Merrell, "The Impact of Unauthorized Immigrants on the Budgets of State and Local Governments." Congressional Budget Office, Last modified December 2007. Accessed October 16, 2011. http://www.cbo.gov/ftpdocs/87xx/doc8711/12-6-Immigration.pdf.

[52] Ibid.

[53] Damien Cave, "Better Lives for Mexicans Cut Allure of Going North." New York Times, July 6, 2011. Accessed October 15, 2011. http://www.nytimes.com/interactive/2011/07/06/world/americas/immigration.html.

[54] U.S. Department of State. "Background Note: Mexico." U.S. Department of State, Last modified December 14, 2010. Accessed October 10, 2011. http://www.state.gov/r/pa/ei/bgn/35749.htm.

[55] Organization for Economic Co-operation and Development. "OECD Economic Surveys: Mexico."

[56] Gustavo Guerra, "Mexico: Children's Rights – August 2007." Law Library of Congress, Last modified August 2007. Accessed October 13, 2011. http://www.loc.gov/law/help/child-rights/pdfs/childrensrights-mexico.pdf.

[57] Yolanda K. Kodrzycki, "Educational Attainment as a Constraint on Economic Growth."

[58] Lance Lochner, National Bureau of Economic Research, "Education Policy and Crime," 34.

[59] Organization for Economic Co-operation and Development. "OECD Economic Surveys: Mexico."

BIBLIOGRAPHY

Alliance for Excellent Education, "Saving Futures, Saving Dollars, The Impact of Education on Crime Reduction and Earnings." Last modified August, 2006. Accessed October 14, 2011. http://www.all4ed.org/files/SavingFutures.pdf

Alsalam, Nabeel, and Jonathan Schwabish. "A Description of the Immigrant Population:." Congress of the United States Congressional Budget Office, Last modified June 2011. Accessed October 12, 2022. http://www.cbo.gov/ftpdocs/121xx/doc12168/06-02-Foreign-BornPopulation.pdf.

Cave, Damien. "Better Lives for Mexicans Cut Allure of Going North." New York Times, July 6, 2011. Accessed October 15, 2011. http://www.nytimes.com/interactive/2011/07/06/world/americas/immigration.html.

Center for Immigration Studies. "Poverty and Income." Center for Immigration Studies, Accessed October 12, 2011. http://www.cis.org/articles/2001/mexico/poverty.html.

Central Intelligence Agency. "The World Factbook: Mexico." Central Intelligence Agency, Last modified September 27, 2011. Accessed October 12, 2022. https://www.cia.gov/library/publications/the-world-factbook/geos/mx.html.

De la Luz Arriaga Lemus , Maria. "NAFTA and the Trinational Coalition to Defend Public Education." ResourceLibrary, Last modified October 1999. Accessed October 14, 2011. http://findarticles.com/p/articles/mi_hb3427/is_3_26/ai_n28749669/.

Densley, Ross. "Who's Responsible for U.S. Illegal Drug Traffic." Next Generation Pharmaceutical, Last modified March 18, 2010. Accessed October 15, 2011. http://www.ngpharma.com/news/Whos-responsible-for-US-illegal-drug-traffic/.

Donohue, John, and Peter Siegelman. "Allocating Resources among Prisons and Social." Yale Law School, Last modified 1998. Accessed October 15, 2011. http://digitalcommons.law.yale.edu/cgi/viewcontent.cgi?article=1050&context=fss_papers&sei-redir=1&referer=http%3A%2F%2Fwww.google.com%2Fsearch%3Fq%3DJ.%2BDonohue%2BIII%2Band%2BP.%2BSiegelman.%2BAllocating%2BResources%2BAmong%2BPrisons%2Band%2BSocial%2BPrograms%2Binthe%2BBattle%2BAgainst%2BCrime.%26rls%3Dcom.microsoft%3Aen-us%26ie%3DUTF-8%26oe%3DUTF-8%26startIndex%3D%26startPage%3D1#search=%22J.%20Donohue%20III%20P.%20Siegelman.%20Allocating%20Resources%20Among%20Prisons%20Social%20Programs%20inthe%20Battle%20Against%20Crime.%22

Gibbons, Patrick R. "Does higher education drive our economic growth?." Las Vegas Review Journal, February 27, 2011. Accessed August 15, 2011. http://www.lvrj.com/opinion/does-higher-education-drive-our-economic-growth-117005288.html.

Guerra, Gustavo. "Mexico: Children's Rights – August 2007." Law Library of Congress, Last modified August 2007. Accessed October 13, 2011. http://www.loc.gov/law/help/child-rights/pdfs/childrensrights-mexico.pdf.

Hanushek, Eric A., and Ludger Wößmann. "The Role of Education Quality in Economic Growth." The World Bank, Last modified February 2007. Accessed October 15, 2011. http://library1.nida.ac.th/worldbankf/fulltext/wps04122.pdf.

Kodrzycki, Yolanda K. "EDUCATIONAL ATTAINMENT AS A CONSTRAINT ON." The Federal Reserve Bank of Boston, Last modified June 2002. Accessed October 14, 2011. http://www.oecd.org/dataoecd/35/24/44696802.pdf.

Lochner, Lance. National Bureau of Economic Research, "Education Policy and Crime." Last modified March, 2010. Accessed August 31, 2011. http://economics.uwo.ca/faculty/lochner/papers/educationpolicycrime_mar10.pdf.

Lochner, Lance and Enrico Moretti. "The Effect of Education on Crime: Evidence from Prison Inmates,." Department of Economics, Berkeley, Last modified October 2003. Accessed October 15, 2011. http://www.econ.berkeley.edu/~moretti/lm46.pdf.

López-Acevedo, Gladys. "Evolution of Earnings and Rates of Returns to Education in Mexico." World Bank, Last modified October 2001. Accessed October 14, 2011. http://www.google.com/url?sa=t&source=web&cd=3&sqi=2&ved=0CC8QFjAC&url=http%3A%2F%2Fciteseerx.ist.psu.edu%2Fviewdoc%2Fdownload%3Fdoi%3D10.1.1.17.6364%26rep%3Drep1%26type%3Dpdf&rct=j&q=Lopez%20Acevedo%20%2B%20education%20to%20earnings&ei=CsKYTuXHNIWQsQKWnYypCA&usg=AFQjCNHgEaoO1nSzegZ7Z6mtulapwXjKFw

Merrell, Melissa. "The Impact of Unauthorized Immigrants on the Budgets of State and Local Governments." Congressional Budget Office, Last modified December 2007. Accessed October 16, 2011. http://www.cbo.gov/ftpdocs/87xx/doc8711/12-6-Immigration.pdf.

Organization for Economic Co-operation and Development "Education at a Glance 2009: OECD Indicators." Organization for Economic Co-operation and Development, Last modified 2009. Accessed October 11, 2011. http://www.oecd.org/document/24/0,3746,en_2649_39263238_43586328_1_1_1_1,00.html

Organization for Economic Co-operation and Development. "OECD Economic Surveys: Mexico." Organization for Economic Co-operation and Development, Last modified May 2011. Accessed October 14, 2011. http://www.oecd.org/dataoecd/59/58/47875549.pdf.

Organization for Economic Co-operation and Development. "Policy brief on Mexico: Education." Organization for Economic Co-operation and Development, Last modified 2006. Accessed October 14, 2011. www.foropoliticaspublicas.org.mx/docs/Educacion.pdf.

Organization for Economic Co-operation and Development. "Towards a Teacher Evaluation Framework in Mexico:." Organization for Economic Co-operation and Development, Last modified December 2009. Accessed October 14, 2011. http://www.oecd.org/dataoecd/35/24/44696802.pdf.

Santibañez, Lucrecia, Georges Vernez, and Paula Razquin. RAND, "Education in Mexico, Challenges and Opportunities." Last modified 2005. Accessed August 31, 2011. http://www.worldfund.org/assets/files/rand_education%20in%20mexico.pdf.

Shirk, David A. "The Drug War in Mexico Confronting a Shared Threat." Council on Foreign Relations, Last modified March 2011. Accessed October 12, 2011. i.cfr.org/content/publications/attachments/Mexico_CSR60.pdf.

Stolberg, Sheryl G. "Obama Calls for U.S. to Lead in Graduation." The New York Times, August 9, 2010. Accessed August 15, 2011. http://www.nytimes.com/2010/08/10/education/10obama.html?adxnnl=1&adxnnlx=1318711313-n9A+Zk63f0wvUouNC+RILg.

U.S. Department of State. "Background Note: Mexico." U.S. Department of State, Last modified December 14, 2010. Accessed October 10, 2011. http://www.state.gov/r/pa/ei/bgn/35749.htm.

Villarreal, Angeles. "U.S.-Mexico Economic Relations: Trends, Issues, and Implications." Congressional Research Service, Last modified March 31, 2010. Accessed October 16, 2011. http://www.nationalaglawcenter.org/assets/crs/RL32934.pdf.

www.ingramcontent.com/pod-product-compliance
Lightning Source LLC
Chambersburg PA
CBHW081812280526
45789CB00008B/3107